MW01000068

■SCHOLASTI■

25 Fun Phonics Plays
for Beginning Readers

**Engaging, Reproducible Plays That Target and Teach
Key Phonics Skills—and Get Kids Eager to Read!**

Pamela Chanko

New York • Toronto • London • Auckland • Sydney
Mexico City • New Delhi • Hong Kong • Buenos Aires

Teaching
Resources

5242

Acknowledgements

◆ ◆ ◆ ◆ ◆

Many thanks to Mackie Rhodes, who rescued Sir Drake,
and to Deborah Schecter, who gave Stan and Stella their starring roles.

Edited by Immacula A. Rhodes

Cover design by Jason Robinson

Interior design by Sydney Wright

Interior illustrations by Abby Carter, Anne Kennedy, and Bari Weissman

ISBN-13: 978-0-545-10339-8
ISBN-10: 0-545-10339-8

Published by Scholastic Inc.

4 5 6 7 8 9 10 40 15 14 13 12

Contents

Phonics Plays

SHORT VOWELS

LONG VOWELS

OTHER VOWELS

CONSONANT DIGRAPHS

CONSONANT BLENDS

Introduction

Being a beginning reader is an exciting time in children's lives. The mysteries of the printed word are just beginning to reveal themselves, and children are getting a taste of the independence they crave: the ability to say, "I can read it all by myself." This stage of children's development is also a crucial one for teachers, because it is often at this time that a child's attitude towards reading begins to set. As early readers encounter a larger variety of words in the materials they use, their excitement about reading may be tempered with frustration. The picture clues, familiar sight words, and predictable text patterns that children once relied on are often replaced with more sophisticated text, making reading a greater challenge for them. So, will children come to view reading as a daunting chore or an exhilarating adventure?

Research has shown that direct phonics instruction is an essential component in teaching literacy. As children encounter increasingly more difficult text, they must go beyond using context clues to figure out unfamiliar words and rely more on their ability to decode, or "sound out," the words. Building decoding skills requires readers to know common sound-spelling relationships—in other words, phonics. Given solid phonics instruction, children can develop the skills needed to sound out a large percentage of the words they encounter in their reading. With practice, their ability to recognize those words becomes better—and faster. The outcome? Increased comprehension. The less time children need to focus on decoding words, the more mental energy they can apply to the meaning of the text. Repeated practice with common sound-spelling relationships helps children develop automaticity in word recognition so that they become more fluent readers, which in turn contributes to minimizing their frustration and maximizing their enjoyment of reading.

So, we know that giving children direct phonics instruction is essential; but making it enjoyable is another ball game altogether! Rote practice in learning sound-spelling relationships is far from engaging, and studying lists of words is often unproductive. Without context, phonetic rules are unlikely to stick with children for long; and the context provided by leveled readers with controlled text is sometimes questionable. The language can seem stilted, and plot is often sacrificed in the service of word study. Another way to provide context is by taking advantage of "teachable moments" while children are engaged in non-instructional texts, pointing out specific sound-spelling patterns as they occur naturally. This is a helpful practice, but those teachable moments may not occur as frequently as needed to benefit young readers. One way to solve this problem? *25 Fun Phonics Plays for Beginning Readers*! Each engaging, plot- and character-driven drama in this book focuses on a particular sound, helping to immerse children in its sound-spelling relationships and giving them all the benefits of repeated exposure—without sacrificing the story!

In addition, reading plays can boost children's fluency skills. Practice in reading aloud helps children build confidence, accuracy, and comprehension, while providing teachers with a welcome opportunity for spontaneous assessment. And read-aloud practice works better when there's a reason behind the activity. While round-robin read-alouds, in which each child reads a portion of a text, has some benefits, the genre may not be a natural fit and, often, children's assigned parts can seem random. In contrast, plays are designed to be read aloud, and each child is given a part that he or she can really own. Playing the part of a character gives reading a purpose that truly engages children. Plus, you can assign parts according to children's skill level, giving them just the challenge they need.

The plays in this book do not require backdrops, costumes, props, or any other elaborate setup. All you need is a copier, and you're ready to go! With these plays, children get the combined benefits of phonics instruction and fluency practice as they engage in rich, motivating read-aloud experiences. For example, children will:

❋ learn the short-*o* sound while reading about a frog-hopping contest

❋ practice long *i* as they discover how Mike learns to ride a bike

❋ learn about the "bossy *r*" as they share Turtle and Squirrel's experiences at the circus

❋ practice the consonant blend *sp* as they meet some very special spiders

❋ and much more!

On the following pages, you'll find suggestions on how to make the most of children's play-reading experiences, in addition to hands-on phonics activities and games to reinforce the skills they're learning. So if you thought the words "fun" and "phonics" made an odd pair, think again: with *25 Fun Phonics Plays for Beginning Readers*, they go together like letters and sounds!

Connections to the Language Arts Standards

Mid-continent Research for Education and Learning (McREL), a nationally recognized, nonprofit organization, has compiled and evaluated national and state standards, and proposed what teachers should provide for their students to grow proficient in language arts, among other curriculum areas. The activities in this book support these standards for grades K–2 in the following areas.

Uses the general skills and strategies of the reading process:

• Uses basic elements of phonetic analysis (such as common letter/sound relationships, beginning and ending consonants, vowel sounds, blends, and word patterns) to decode unknown words

• Uses basic elements of structural analysis (such as syllables and spelling patterns) to decode unknown words

• Understands level-appropriate sight words and vocabulary

• Reads aloud familiar stories and passages with fluency and expression

Uses reading skills and strategies to understand and interpret a variety of literary texts:

• Uses reading skills and strategies to understand a variety of familiar literary passages and texts

• Knows the basic characteristics of familiar genres

• Knows setting, main characters, main events, sequence, and problems in stories

Uses listening and speaking strategies for different purposes:

• Uses different voice level, phrasing, and intonation for different situations

• Recites and responds to familiar stories

Source: Kendall, J. S. and Marzano, R. J. (2004). *Content knowledge: A compendium of standards and benchmarks for K–12 education.* Aurora, CO: Mid-continent Research for Education and Learning. Online database: http://www.mcrel.org/standards-benchmarks/

Using the plays...

Use the following tips and ideas to get the most out of using the plays in your classroom.

Before Reading

✳ Make copies of the play for each child who will be reading a part, whether the participants are reading in small groups or as a whole class. The plays range in number of parts from two to enough for the entire class.

✳ You might copy the play onto a transparency for use on an overhead projector, or write the text on chart paper. This way, you can track the print when you first read the text with the group. (You can also use the text on the chart in a phonics mini-lesson with the class.)

✳ Before reading the play, introduce the targeted phonics skill to children. Say the sound aloud and point out (or write) its spelling or spellings. Tell children the sound will appear many times as you read the play, so they should get ready for it!

✳ Assign parts to children according to their skill level. You will find that some roles require a bit more reading than others. You will also find that many of the roles in the plays are flexible: you can have individuals read them, or you might assign a group of children to each role and have them read the part chorally. For instance, in *Blue Jay's Birthday Surprise* (page 22), individual children can read the roles of Snake, Ape, and Snail or small groups might read the parts for the animals.

✳ Once children have their assigned roles, provide them with highlighter pens so they can mark their lines. This will make it easier for children to find their character's parts as the group reads the play.

During Reading

✳ When introducing the play, you may want to read all of the text aloud to children, as you would any other story. This will familiarize children with the language, characters, and plot. First, read the play straight through for enjoyment. On the second reading, you can focus on the phonics element by inviting children to signal when they hear the target sound (for instance, by raising their hand). You can also pause to point out different spellings of the phonetic element, if appropriate.

✳ You can follow any format you'd like to have children read the plays. You might conduct an informal reading, in which every child has a script and reads his or her part in turn. Or, a small group might sit in a corner of the room to read the play in a literature circle. A cast of characters could stand up before the class and read the

25 Fun Phonics Plays for Beginning Readers © 2009 by Pamela Chanko, Scholastic Teaching Resources

play aloud in a reader's theater performance. The class audience might simply watch the performance, or they might follow along using their own copies of the play.

✳ Another option is to break the class up into small reading groups. Assign each group a play (or a phonetic element). Have the groups practice their plays simultaneously. Then, when everyone is ready, the class can put on a "recital," with one group reading after another. For a fun extra challenge, members of the class audience can try to count how many times the target sound occurs in each group's performance!

✳ There may be some members of your group who are self-conscious or feel uncomfortable when performing in front of others. Using simple stick puppets and a makeshift stage might help ease the performance anxieties of these children and add to the fun for everyone. Simply cover a table with a long tablecloth for children to kneel behind as they use their puppets to act out the roles of their characters. This will help children feel more secure—and less exposed—as they perform the play.

After Reading

✳ You might consider recording children as they read the plays and then put the recording in the listening center, along with a copy of the play. Children will thrill to hearing their own voices as they follow along with the text!

✳ Have children use highlighter pens to mark all the words with the target sound on their copies of the play. When finished, invite them to read the play again. During this reading, ask children to emphasize each highlighted word as they come to it. You might also highlight words with the target sound on a transparency of the play. Display the transparency on an overhead projector and use it to help children identify the spelling of the target sound in each highlighted word.

✳ Make copies of the plays for children to take home and read with family members. You can even include a letter inviting families to do a quick related activity with their child. For instance, if you send home a copy of *The Thunderstorm* (page 45), you might invite them to write down the number of words starting with *th* that they hear on a half-hour television program.

✳ Why not put on a production at school and invite family and friends? There's no need for Broadway-caliber sets and costumes; a few simple props will do. For example, a small blanket and throw pillow for snuggling, plus a pot and a spoon to stir up some pretend snow-pea soup, are all you need to perform *Snail Has the Sniffles* (page 56). And some play food and dishes are more than enough to put on a full-scale production of *Flea's Tea Party* (page 25). Children will have their own ideas as well, so let their creativity blossom. Then send out flyers and show families how much fun phonics can be!

Fun Phonics Activities

Use these fun, hands-on activities and games to get kids excited about phonics and make target sound-spellings stick!

Follow That Sound!

Scavenger hunts are great fun—in print or in the classroom.

❋ To reinforce the spellings of targeted sounds, set up a learning center with a stack of old magazines, scissors, glue, and sheets of large construction paper. Invite children to look through the magazines for words that begin with the spelling (or spellings) for a particular sound. Have them cut out the words and glue them to construction paper to make a colorful collage.

❋ For a more kinesthetic activity, children can search the classroom or school building to find objects that contain their assigned sound. For instance, if children are learning the *cl* blend, they might find a *clock, closet, clip, clothespin*, and, of course, *classmates!* Have children write the names of their findings on index cards and post them on a phonics word wall.

Silly Sentences

Studying initial sounds is perfect for tongue-twister fun!

❋ Encourage children to look and listen for examples of alliteration as they read the plays. Then take advantage of learning words with common sounds by challenging children to make up their own silly alliterative sentences—in other words, tongue twisters!

❋ Write words that begin with your target consonant, blend, or digraph (for example, *pr*) on separate index cards. Then place the index cards on a table and have children work together to arrange them into a sentence, adding words as needed for sense. For example: *Pretty princesses proudly practice prancing with pretzels on the prairie!*

Swat-a-Sound

This game, which lets you use your regular classroom word wall, requires fast reflexes plus sound-spelling recognition!

1. Divide the class into two teams and have the teams line up a short distance from your word wall.

2. Give the first child in each line a fly swatter and have that child step up to the wall. Then call out a sound to swat. That's it! The instruction can be as simple or as detailed as you like, depending on the target skills you're teaching. Here are some examples:

25 Fun Phonics Plays for Beginning Readers © 2009 by Pamela Chanko, Scholastic Teaching Resources

Swat a short a word; Swat a word that ends with the sound /ch/; Swat a word that has the sound /st/ in the middle.

3. The first child to swat a correct word (there may be more than one) earns a point for his or her team. You can play until each child has had a turn, or as time permits.

What's My Sound?

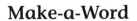

This mix 'n' mingle party game is sure to keep children guessing!

1. Write target sounds on sticky notes, one for each child. Use a different sound-spelling on each card, for instance, *dr, g, oo, th*, and so on. Then place a sticky note on each child's back, making sure children cannot see their own sounds.

2. Let children mill about the classroom, asking one another questions to try to figure out what sound-spelling is on their back! The one rule is that children may only ask yes or no questions. For example, a child might ask: *Does my sound help you say* balloon? or *Is it the first letter in* gorilla? But children may not ask questions such as: *What words can you say with my sound?*

3. Encourage children to keep playing even after they have guessed their own sound. They can remain in the game to provide other children with clues.

Make-a-Word

With this game, children practice initial consonants, digraphs, and blends, long and short vowels, and word-building skills!

1. Get two empty tissue boxes, cube-shaped, and cover them in plain construction paper. On one cube, write target initial consonants, digraphs, and blends, such as *s, p, b, st, ch, tr*. On the other cube, write common word endings, featuring both long and short vowels. Include endings that will form several words when combined with the initial sounds you chose, for example: *eat, ain, oke, it, un, ack*.

2. Gather children in a circle to play the game. Each player takes a turn tossing the cubes like dice. If the player can form a word with the initial sound and word ending that the two cubes land on, the player gets one point. If not, but another player can form a word, that player earns the point. (Players may also challenge the legitimacy of a word; children should have a dictionary nearby.)

3. Children continue until a specified number of points is reached, or as time permits.

Dropcloth Phonics

Use an old sheet or a shower curtain for lots of phonics fun!

✳ Use a permanent marker to draw rows of large circles on your cloth. Inside each circle, write the spelling for a target sound. Repeat some of the same sounds that are spelled different ways. For instance, you might use *ai, ay,* and *a_e* for the long *a* sound; *ee, e_e,* and *ea* for long *e*; and *y, igh,* and *i_e* for long *i*. You can

also include consonants, blends, and digraphs. Place the cloth on the floor in an open area, and you have a giant game board to play two different phonics games!

✳ For the first game, children will need a beanbag. Tape a line on the floor a short distance away from the game board (use masking tape). Then have children stand behind the line and take turns tossing the beanbag onto the cloth. When their beanbag lands on a spelling, ask children to say the sound. Depending on their skill level, you can then have children name a word that contains that sound and uses that spelling for an extra point. Play as long as time permits.

✳ For the second game, be prepared for lots of laughter! Use the multiple vowel spellings for a phonics version of Twister™! Call out instructions such as *Right hand on long a! Left foot on long i! Right foot on long e!* Children must place the appropriate body part on any spelling that makes the named sound. Doubtless, some children will collapse in giggles. The last child on the mat who has both hands and feet on spellings of called-out sounds should be very proud—both physically and phonetically!

We Go Together

Play this game when you need children to form groups—or anytime!

1. On separate index cards, write words that have common target sounds. Choose words that spell the sound differently or have the sound in a different position. For instance, if your target sound is long *a*, you might create a group of five cards with the words *cake, hay, tape, pain,* and *they*. If your target sound is /ch/, you might create cards with the words *chip, beach, munch, chunk,* and *chew.* Create enough cards for each child to have one, making sure each child will be part of a group. To create a checking system, color-code each set of words by placing sticker dots on the back of the cards.

2. Punch two holes in the top of each card and string with yarn to make a necklace. Then give each child a necklace to wear, words facing out.

3. Let children walk around looking at one another's words, searching for others with whom they have a sound in common. Remind children that in order to form a group, all members must have words that contain the same target sound.

4. Once children have gathered into their groups, have them turn their cards over to see if their stickers match!

Sam and Cam's Snack

Characters

Sam   Alex
Cam

Sam: I am hungry, Cam.

Cam: Me, too, Sam.
            What shall we have?

Sam: We have a bag of snacks.
            It should be on the rack.
            I will grab it.

Cam: I will give you a hand.

Sam: Oh, no! The bag is gone!

Cam: That makes me mad!

Sam: Me, too! Where can it be?

Cam: Is it in back of the jam?

Sam: No! Is it in that basket of yams?

Cam: No! Is it behind the crackers?

Sam: No! Could it be in the trash?

Cam: I am so hungry, I can't stand it.
I need to eat fast!

Sam: Let's get the facts.
Who had a snack last?

Cam: I did. But I put the bag back.

Sam: It just doesn't add up.
We will catch the rat who took it!

Cam: Yes! Let's plan a trap!

Alex: Hi, Sam and Cam.
Did you know that your cat is out?
She's over there in the grass.
And she's dragging a bag!

Sam: It's the snack sack!
Catch that cat!

Cam: Don't let her get past you!
Thanks, Alex! You're a pal!

Alex: It was a snap! I'm glad to help.

Sam: At last, we can eat!
Here, have a snack.

Alex: Even the cat?

Cam: Sure! Cats need snacks, too!

The End

25 Fun Phonics Plays for Beginning Readers © 2009 by Pamela Chanko, Scholastic Teaching Resources

The Best Pet

Characters

Benji	Jed	Mom
Etta	Penny	Dad

Benji: My parents are getting me a pet!

Etta: What kind of pet will you get?

Benji: I don't know yet.
What's the best pet to get?

Jed: Get a hen.
You could help her build a nest.

Penny: She will give you fresh eggs.

Etta: You can eat them for breakfast!

Benji: No, feathers make a mess.
And hens peck too much.

Penny: Then how about an elephant?

Etta: You could build a tent for him.

Jed: And sell rides for ten cents!

Benji: No, an elephant is too heavy.
How would I get him to the vet?

Etta:	Well, how about a penguin?
Jed:	You could sled together in the snow!
Benji:	No, my parents would never let me. Let's just forget it.
Jed, Etta, and Penny:	We are trying to help, Benji. What pet do you want?
Benji:	I want a pet that will be my friend.
Mom:	Hi, Benji! We got you a pet.
Penny:	It's a yellow kitten!
Dad:	It's a kitten that needs a friend.
Jed, Etta, and Penny:	Benji can be her friend!
Benji:	Yes! We will be the best friends ever!

☀ The End ☀

25 Fun Phonics Plays for Beginning Readers © 2009 by Pamela Chanko, Scholastic Teaching Resources

Piggy's Picnic

Piggy: It is spring!
Let's have a picnic.

Tigger: Where will it be?

Piggy: On the hill!

Digger: What will we bring?

Piggy: Let's make a list.

Tigger: I will bring dishes.

Digger: I will bring napkins.

Piggy: I will bring a quilt to sit on.
But I will not bring my kid sister.

Tigger and Digger: Why not?

Piggy: She sticks to me like glue.
I can't get rid of her!

Tigger
and Digger: We think she is nice.
But it is up to you.

Piggy: I will see you at the picnic.

Piggy, Tigger,
and Digger: At last, it is picnic time!

Tigger: I brought the dishes.

Digger: I brought the napkins.

Piggy: I brought a quilt to sit on.
But something is missing.

Tigger: What is it?
We made a list.
What did we forget?

Digger: We forgot one thing.
But it is not on the list.

Piggy, Tigger,
and Digger: FOOD!

Tigger: And drinks!
I'm thirsty!

Digger: I wish we had tuna fish.

Tigger: I wish we had chips.

Piggy: I wish we had milk.

Digger: I wish we had put
those things on our list!

- - - - - - →

25 Fun Phonics Plays for Beginning Readers © 2009 by Pamela Chanko, Scholastic Teaching Resources

Tigger: Look! It's Piggy's kid sister.

Kid Sister: Piggy, can I come to your picnic?
I brought food and drinks.
I brought some for everyone.

Piggy: You did?

**Tigger
and Digger:** Piggy's kid sister saved the day!

Piggy: Thank you, Sis!
From this day on,
I will be a better big sister!

✳ The End ✳

The Hopping Frog Contest

Characters

Spotted Frog   Bog Frog

Spotted Frog: Can I sit on your log?

Bog Frog: Sure. Hop on.

Spotted Frog: This is a nice pond.

Bog Frog: Yes, I like it a lot.

Spotted Frog: It is hot today!

Bog Frog: Why don't you hop
into the water?

Spotted Frog: Yes, why not?
I was the best hopper
at my old pond.

Bog Frog: Well, I am the best hopper
at this pond.

Spotted Frog: Let's have a hopping contest.

Bog Frog: All right.

Spotted Frog: Watch me hop.
Plop!

Bog Frog:	I can top that! Watch me hop! Plop!
Spotted Frog:	So! I can do a flip-flop! Flop!
Bog Frog:	Well, watch me dive and drop! Drop!
Spotted Frog:	I can jog on these rocks.
Bog Frog:	I can trot on these logs.
Spotted Frog and Bog Frog:	I'm getting tired. I want to stop.
Spotted Frog:	That was fun! We both did a good job.
Bog Frog:	Let's call the contest a tie.
Spotted Frog:	We are both top hoppers!
Bog Frog:	I'm still hot.
Spotted Frog:	Let's pop back into the water.
Spotted Frog and Bog Frog:	Kerplop!

✳ The End ✳

Hush, Puppy!

Characters

Puppy   Cub
Bunny   Duckling

Puppy: I am just a puppy!
            I want to stay up!

**Bunny, Cub,
and Duckling:**   Hush, Puppy!
            It's time for bed.

Puppy: But I want to run!

Bunny: Hush, Puppy!
            We tucked you in.

Puppy: But I want to jump in a puddle!

Cub: Hush, Puppy!
            We hummed you to sleep.

Puppy: But I want to tug my toy truck!

Duckling: Hush, Puppy!
            Shut your eyes.

Puppy: But I want to have fun!

     25 Fun Phonics Plays for Beginning Readers © 2009 by Pamela Chanko, Scholastic Teaching Resources

Bunny: Hush, Puppy!
Just wait until the sun comes up.

Puppy: But I want bubble gum!

Cub: Hush, Puppy!
Must you make such a fuss?

Puppy: But I want a cup of tea!

Duckling: Hush, Puppy!
Don't make so much noise.

Puppy: But I want to ride the bus!

**Bunny, Cub,
and Duckling:** Hush, Puppy!
You are keeping us all up!

Bunny: Silly us!
We know what Puppy really wants!

Cub: A hug!
And a tummy rub!

Duckling: There. Now he is snug.

**Bunny, Cub,
and Duckling:** Are you asleep, Puppy?

Puppy: Almost. Hush!

✳ The End ✳

Blue Jay's Birthday

Characters

Snake   Blue Jay   Friends
Ape   Snail

Snake: Pssst!
Blue Jay is coming this way.

Ape: Tell him to stay away.

Blue Jay: Today is my birthday!
I came to play.

Snake, Ape, and Snail: Blue Jay, go away!

Blue Jay: That was mean to say!
You made me sad.
I will go away.

Snail: Hey, that was close!

Ape: Did Blue Jay see the cake
that you baked?

Snake: No, we hid it under the table.

Ape: Great! You saved the day!

   *25 Fun Phonics Plays for Beginning Readers* © 2009 by Pamela Chanko, Scholastic Teaching Resources

Snail: Are all our plans in place?
Let's make sure.
Is the name on the cake?

Snake: Yes! Hooray!
Are the plates on the table?

Ape: Yes! Hooray!
Are the games set up to play?

Snail: Yes! Hooray!
Do our friends know the date?

Snake, Ape, and Snail: Yes! Hooray!

Friends: Today is the day!
Are we late?
Is Blue Jay here?

Snail: We're waiting for him.

Ape: Pssst!
Blue Jay is coming this way.

Snake: He's walking down the lane.

Snail: Everyone, hide!

Ape: Shhhh!
Don't make a sound.

Blue Jay: I came back to play.
Snake. Ape. Snail.
Where is everyone? - - - - ->

Snake, Ape, Snail, and Friends: Surprise, Blue Jay!
Happy Birthday!

Blue Jay: What a happy day!
This is the greatest
birthday party ever!

Snake, Ape, Snail, and Friends: We're glad you came!
And now, we want you to stay!

All: Hooray!

✳ The End ✳

25 Fun Phonics Plays for Beginning Readers © 2009 by Pamela Chanko, Scholastic Teaching Resources

Flea's Tea Party

Characters

Bee	Deer	Flea
Zebra	Sheep	

Bee and Zebra: We are here
for Flea's tea party.

Deer and Sheep: So are we.

Flea: Have a seat.

Bee: Wow! What a feast!

Zebra: This is a meal for a queen!

Sheep: Look at all these treats!

Deer: It looks too pretty to eat!

Flea: Gee, don't worry.
It was easy.
Do you want tea?

**Bee, Zebra,
Deer, and Sheep:** Yes, please.

Bee: Pass the peach pie.

Sheep: I need the cookies, please.

Deer: Can you reach the green beans?

Zebra: Please pass the cheese.

Flea: You were really hungry.

Bee, Zebra, Deer, and Sheep: And thirsty!
More tea, please!

Flea: Here you are.

Bee and Zebra: What a great party!
We need to go now.

Sheep and Zebra: We must leave, too.
We'll see you soon!

Flea: I've never seen such a mess.
It will take me a week
to clean up!

Bee, Zebra, Deer, and Sheep: We came back, Flea.
We could not leave you
to clean your house alone.

Flea: How sweet!
Here's a broom.
Start sweeping!

* The End *

Mike Rides a Bike

Characters

Mike	Ivy
Spike	Liza

Mike: Hi, Spike.
Do you like my new bike?

Spike: Yes! It's really nice.
I like the bright red stripes.

Mike: It's the nicest bike I could find.

Spike: Is it fun to ride?

Mike: I don't know.
I haven't tried.

Spike: Why?

Mike: I never rode a bike in my life!

Spike: Then it's about time!
Climb on!

Mike: This is nice! I'm riding!
Oh no! I'm sliding!
I'm falling!

Ivy and Liza: Are you all right?

Mike: I'm fine.

Ivy: We were passing by.

Liza: And we heard a cry.

Spike: Mike is learning how to ride a bike.

Ivy and Liza: We know the right way to ride.
We can teach you, Mike.

Mike: You don't mind?
That's very kind.

Ivy: Here, try it like this.

Mike: Here I go. YIKES!
Right onto the sidewalk!

Liza: Try again, Mike.

Spike: You have to practice a long time.

Mike: Okay, I'll try again.
Hey! I can ride! I can ride!

Spike, Ivy, and Liza: Look at Mike fly by!
We knew he could ride!
He just had to try . . .

Mike: And try, and try . . .

All: And try!

✳ The End ✳

25 Fun Phonics Plays for Beginning Readers © 2009 by Pamela Chanko, Scholastic Teaching Resources

Is It a Snow Day?

Characters

Bo	Omar
Toby	Josie

Bo: Is it a snow day?

Toby: Can we stay home?

Omar: The snow's been falling fast!

Josie: It's been snowing since I woke up!

Bo: It won't slow down!

Toby: I hope we don't have to go to school!

Omar: How will we know?

Josie: Someone will say so on the radio.

Toby: The whole back yard looks white.

Josie: The oak tree looks white, too!

Bo: It's hard to see out the window.
There is so much snow on it.

Omar: How cold is it?

Toby: It's cold enough
to freeze your nose!

Josie: It's cold enough
to freeze your toes!

Bo: It may even be below zero.

Toby: Then we can't go to school.

Omar: Why?

Toby: We can't go outside.
We would catch a cold!

Josie: Hey! It is a snow day!
It was on the radio!
And mom just said so!

Toby: Everybody, get your coat!

Omar, Josie, and Bo: Why?

Toby: So we can go roll in the snow!

Omar, Josie, and Bo: Won't you catch a cold, Toby?

Toby: Oh, no! Not on a snow day!

✳ The End ✳

25 Fun Phonics Plays for Beginning Readers © 2009 by Pamela Chanko, Scholastic Teaching Resources

Hugo's Unicorn

Characters

Hugo   Dad
Mom

Hugo: Mom! Dad!
I just saw a unicorn!

Mom: Unicorns don't go out to eat, Hugo.

Dad: Hugo, look at your menu.

Hugo: You never believe me.
It's no use.

Mom: The music will start soon.
We need to go.

Hugo: There goes the unicorn again!
Its horn was huge!

Dad: Unicorns don't listen to music, Hugo.

Mom: Hugo, I am not amused.

Hugo: You never believe me.
It's no use.

Dad: Don't argue with your mom.
It's time for the museum now. - - - - - - ➔

Hugo: Hey! There's the unicorn!

Mom: Unicorns don't look at art, Hugo.
Stop being cute.

Hugo: It just ran around the corner!

Dad: There are no such things as unicorns.

Mom: Oh! Here is a unicorn.
But this is just a painting, Hugo.

Hugo: No! It's real!
You never believe me!
It's no use!

Dad: Sorry, Hugo.
Let's go home.

Hugo: What is it, Mom?
You look confused.

Mom: I was thinking about that painting.
It was very unusual.

Dad: How so?

Mom: I'm sure that unicorn winked at me!

Dad: Oh no, not this again.

Hugo: Don't worry, Mom.
I believe you!

✳ The End ✳

25 Fun Phonics Plays for Beginning Readers © 2009 by Pamela Chanko, Scholastic Teaching Resources

Sue's Loose Tooth

Characters

Sue	Drew
June	Lou

Sue: I have a loose tooth!

June: Cool!

Drew: The tooth fairy will come soon.

Sue: I might ask for a flute or a tuba.

June: I would ask for blue shoes.

Lou: I would ask for a kangaroo!

Drew: What can Sue do with a kangaroo?

Lou: She can ride it to school.

Drew: I would ask for a hula-hoop.

Sue: Well, I don't have to choose yet.
My tooth just got loose today.

June: There's a way to make it looser.

Drew: Just eat gooey food.

Lou: Let's meet for lunch tomorrow at noon.

All: See everybody soon!

Sue: It's time for lunch.
I have great news!
The tooth fairy flew
into my room last night!

Lou: No way!

June: It had to be the moon in your window.

Sue: No, it was the tooth fairy!
She said my tooth
will come out this afternoon!

Drew: Can that be true?

Lou: Here, Sue.
Have some stew.

Sue: This stew is too chewy.
Oops! My tooth!

June: Woo-hoo!
Sue's tooth came out!

Lou: But was it the food?
Or was it the tooth fairy?

Sue: Who knows?
But watch for me tomorrow.
I may be riding a kangaroo to school!

❋ The End ❋

25 Fun Phonics Plays for Beginning Readers © 2009 by Pamela Chanko, Scholastic Teaching Resources

The Grouchy Groundhog

Characters

Narrator	Groundhog	Mouse
Brown Cow	Owl	

Narrator: Groundhog was always grouchy.
Brown Cow came to cheer him up.
She pounded on the door.

Brown Cow: Groundhog, let me in!

Groundhog: Stop the loud sounds!
Brown Cow, please go away.

Brown Cow: I brought a crown for you.
You can act like you rule the town.
Then you won't be grouchy!

Groundhog: A crown will not take my frown away.

Narrator: Next, Owl shouted at the door.

Owl: Groundhog, let me in!

Groundhog: Owl, please close your mouth!
You're too loud!

Owl: I brought a clown for you.
You two can clown around.
Then you won't be grouchy!

Groundhog: A clown will not take my frown away.

Narrator: Then Mouse came to the house.

Mouse: Groundhog, how are you?
Please come out.

Groundhog: I am grouchy, as always!

Mouse: I came to take you outside.

Groundhog: How will that help me?

Mouse: Come out and see.

Groundhog: The flowers and clouds are beautiful!

Mouse: Why do you pout around the house?
That would make anyone grouchy.
You need to get out and about.

Groundhog: You are right.
Getting out takes my frown away.
From now on, I will get out each day.

Narrator: After that, Groundhog still frowned.
But the world around him was beautiful!
So it was hard to stay grouchy for long.

✳ The End ✳

25 Fun Phonics Plays for Beginning Readers © 2009 by Pamela Chanko, Scholastic Teaching Resources

Turtle's First Circus

Characters

Squirrel   Turtle

Squirrel: Turtle, it's Thursday!
We are going to the circus!

Turtle: I'm scared, Squirrel.

Squirrel: What for? Don't worry.
Here we are.

Turtle: Why is it so dark in here?

Squirrel: The show is about to start.

Turtle: I hear a herd of elephants!
I'm going under my shell!

Squirrel: Turtle, come out of there.
The elephants are part of the show.

Turtle: But horses are marching over here!
I'm going back under!

Squirrel: Turtle, come out.
Here, I'll share my popcorn.

Turtle: Oh! Do you see that girl whirl in the air?
She will get hurt!
I'm going back under!

Squirrel: For the third time . . .
Turtle, come out of there!
You will miss the best show on earth!

Turtle: Hey, is that a bear on a chair?

Squirrel: Yes! She's the star of the show!

Turtle: Look at her twirl in her purple shirt!

Squirrel: She's a very smart bear.
But wait! It gets better.

Turtle: The lions can jump
through a circle of fire!
They don't even burn their fur!

Squirrel: Are you glad you came out after all?

Turtle: Oh, yes!
That was the best circus ever!
Let's come back tomorrow for more!

Squirrel: Sorry, Turtle.
The circus comes only once a year.
But it's worth the wait!

✳ The End ✳

25 Fun Phonics Plays for Beginning Readers © 2009 by Pamela Chanko, Scholastic Teaching Resources

Pete's Pancake House

Characters

Steve	Aunt Dale	Pete
Uncle Joe	Jane	

Steve: I hate long car rides!

Uncle Joe: The drive to see Granny Rose is really quite nice.

Aunt Dale: Why don't we play a game?

Jane: I would like to eat!

Uncle Joe: There's no place to stop. Let's tell some jokes.

Steve: I'm hungry, too. I ate only a few grapes.

Aunt Dale: But we are so close. Let's sing a tune.

Jane: Stop! I see a place! It's "Pete's Pancake House!"

Steve: Can we stop, please?

Uncle Joe: Fine, I give up. Let's go inside.

Pete: Welcome! I'm Pete.
How about a plate of pancakes?

**Uncle Joe
and Aunt Dale:** Delicious!
More, please!

Jane: Thanks for the pancakes, Pete.

Pete: I'm glad you came. Bye!

Aunt Dale: We are late.
Drive fast, Joe!

Steve: We're here.
There's Granny Rose!

Jane: She's at the gate.
Look! She has a huge cake!

Uncle Joe: I couldn't eat one more bite!

Aunt Dale: But we have to taste it.

Steve: Well, I hope you two learned a lesson.

**Uncle Joe
and Aunt Dale:** What's that?

**Steve
and Jane:** Always save room for cake!

* The End *

25 Fun Phonics Plays for Beginning Readers © 2009 by Pamela Chanko, Scholastic Teaching Resources

Chocolate Chip Surprise

ch

> **Characters**
>
> Chuck   Mom
> Chelsea

Chuck: Mom is tired after work each day.
Let's pitch in and make dinner.

Chelsea: We don't know how to cook!

Chuck: The cookbook will teach us.

Chelsea: Here's a chicken recipe.

Chuck: We don't have chicken.
I'll use this cheese instead.

Chelsea: I think that's cheating.

Chuck: It's not such a big deal.
What's next?

Chelsea: Let me check.
Do we have chopped carrots?

Chuck: No. Let's use these cherries.

Chelsea: That doesn't match the recipe.

Chuck: So? Our recipe will be much better!

Chelsea: Then let's put in chocolate chips.

Chuck: And a pinch of pepper. Ah-choo!

Chelsea: Here's are some peaches. Catch!

Chuck: I found chili left over from lunch.
I need a chair to reach it.

Chelsea: Watch out!
The peaches fell!
Boy, this kitchen is a mess.

Mom: I'm home, children!
What is all this?

Chuck and Chelsea: It's called "Chocolate Chip Surprise!"

All: Chomp. Crunch. Munch. YUCK!

Chuck: Sorry, Mom.

Mom: It's the thought that counts.

Chelsea: We'll clean the kitchen.

Mom: Then we'll make sandwiches—together!

Chuck and Chelsea: Three cheers for Mom!

❋ The End ❋

25 Fun Phonics Plays for Beginning Readers © 2009 by Pamela Chanko, Scholastic Teaching Resources

Shark's Wish

Shrimp: Shark, why are you so sad?

Shark: I wish I had more friends.

Shrimp: What do you mean?

Shark: When I smiled at Goldfish,
she dashed away!

Shrimp: Well, you do have sharp teeth.

Shark: I can't help the shape of my teeth!

Shrimp: I know. It's a shame.

Shark: When I'm around,
Goldfish swishes away.
Jellyfish shakes.
Starfish rushes back to shore.

Shrimp: They are just foolish, Shark.

Shark: They are afraid because I'm big.
What shall I do? - - - - - - ➤

Shrimp: Well, I'm short and small.
But you don't push me around.
We can show them how nice you are.

Shark: But I'm so shy!

Shrimp: Hush! You'll be a smash!
Come, sea animals.
Let's have a meeting.

**Goldfish,
Jellyfish,
and Starfish:** We're here!

Shrimp: You should not be afraid of Shark.
He is my friend.
He shares his seashells with me!

Shark: It's true.
I'm not scary.
I'm just shy.

Goldfish: That is a shock!

Starfish: Gosh! We're sorry, Shark.

Jellyfish: Let's be friends!

Shrimp: So, Shark, did your wish come true?

Shark: Yes! Now I have more friends to
share my seashells with!

✳ The End ✳

The Thunderstorm

Characters

Beth   Theo

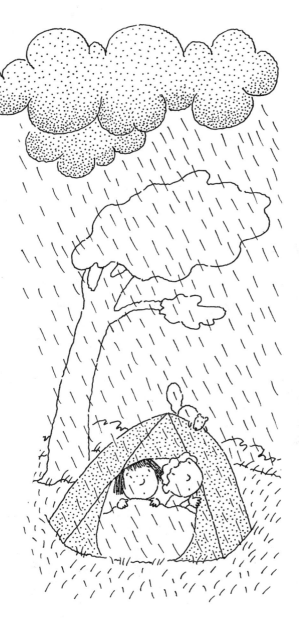

Beth: This camping trip is fun, Theo.

Theo: I think so, too, Beth.

Beth: What was that?

Theo: What?

Beth: I thought I heard something.

Theo: Was it those dripping sounds?

Beth: It must be raining.
It's a good thing we're in this tent!

Theo: It's better than being outside.
But I wish the weather was nice.

Beth: Oh, no! I hear thunder!

Theo: Do you hear that thumping?
The rain is falling down hard!

Beth: Get under these thick blankets.

Theo: Thanks.

Beth: Did you hear that thud?

Theo: It was more like a thunk.
I think a branch fell off a tree!

Beth: Mother and Father must be
worried to death.

Theo: They must be scared for both of us.

Beth: To tell the truth, I'm scared, too!

Theo: Me, too.
I can't catch my breath!

Beth: The tent is rocking back and forth!

Theo: I know we wanted to stay out all night.
But there is a place we can go.

Beth: Are you thinking what I'm thinking?

Theo: I think so.

Beth: Then run! Get inside!

Both: We made it!

Theo: Do you think we'll ever go camping
farther than our backyard?

Beth: Why should we?
There's no place like home!

✳ The End ✳

   25 Fun Phonics Plays for Beginning Readers © 2009 by Pamela Chanko, Scholastic Teaching Resources

A Day at Whiz-Bang Park

Characters

Wally   William
Wanda   Wendy

Wally: Here we are at Whiz-Bang Park!
         Look at all the rides!

Wanda: Which one should we try first?

William: Let's go on the White Whale.
         It's a giant roller coaster!

Wendy: Where is it?

Wally: This map shows the whole park.
         The White Whale is over there.

Wanda: We are nowhere near it.

William: Then let's start walking.
         I can't wait to ride it!

Wendy: Mmm!
         I just got a whiff of hot dogs!

Wally: Let's stop to eat. ------->

William: Eat it while we walk.
Come on.

Wally: Whoops! I dropped it.
I told you to stop!

William: Oh, don't whine.
Wait until you see the White Whale!

Wanda: Look, bumper cars!
Let's give them a whirl.

Wendy: Whoa!
They look like fun!

Wally: Look how they whip around!
Let's all drive.

William: But when will we go
on the White Whale?

Wanda: Who cares?
Get behind the wheel!

All: WHEE! WHOOSH!
WHAM! WHACK!

William: Whew!
You guys were right.
That was fun!

Wendy: Look!
There's the White Whale!

Wally: It's a whopper! - - - - - ➔

 25 Fun Phonics Plays for Beginning Readers © 2009 by Pamela Chanko, Scholastic Teaching Resources

William: Uh, it looks . . . uh . . .

Wanda: Don't whisper!
We can't hear you.
What is it?

William: It looks so scary!
I don't know whether I can go on!

Wally: It does look very scary.

Wendy: I agree.

Wanda: Let's skip it.

All: We still had a whale of a time!

✷ The End ✷

Cliff's Closet

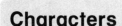

Characters

Cliff   Clay
Closet   Claire

Cliff: Look at the clock!
I need to go to sleep.

Closet: Clink. Clank.

Cliff: I need to rest
for the class spelling bee!

Closet: Clunk. Clonk.

Cliff: I also have a book club
meeting tomorrow!

Closet: Clink, clank, clunk.

Cliff: Those noises are in my closet!
What if it's a monster with claws?

Closet: Clatter!

Cliff: Clay! Get in here, quick!

Closet: Click-clack!

Clay: What's up, little brother?

    25 Fun Phonics Plays for Beginning Readers © 2009 by Pamela Chanko, Scholastic Teaching Resources

Cliff: There's a monster in my closet!

Clay: Stop clowning around.

Closet: Clip-clop-clang!

Clay: What was THAT?

Cliff: It's the monster!

Clay: I'll check the closet.
All I see is clothes.
Wait! There's a pair of clogs . . .
with feet in them!

**Cliff
and Clay:** Claire! Is that you, big sister?

Claire: I was looking for my hair clip.
I thought I left it back there.

Clay: You're so clumsy!
We thought you were a monster!

Claire: I'm not clumsy!
It's all the clutter in your closet!

Cliff: Well, I don't mind the clutter.
But I do mind the monsters!

✳ The End ✳

Sir Drake and the Dragon

Characters

Narrator   People   Sir Drake
Dragon   Prince   Princess

Narrator: A huge dragon lived in Drab.
The people were afraid of him.

Dragon: ROAR!

People: It's the dragon!
We wish we could drive him away!

Narrator: One night, a man rode into town.
He was dripping wet.

Prince: Who are you?

Sir Drake: I am Sir Drake.
May I come in to get dry?

Princess: Yes. Drape your coat by this fire.
Tell me, why have you come to Drab?

Sir Drake: I'm here to fix your dragon problem.

Prince: How can you fix it?
The dragon drops in whenever he wants.

Princess: He drags his tail and knocks things over.

People: He drinks all the water from our wells!

Sir Drake: I know what to do.

Dragon: ROAR!

Sir Drake: Hello, Dragon.
Why do you make the town dread you?

Dragon: Because the people want to drive me away.

Sir Drake: Well, I have come to change that.

Narrator: Sir Drake and Dragon got busy.
They had a lot to do!

Prince: Look! Dragon is dressing up the town!

Princess: Oh, my! He's not dragging his tail.

People: He's drawing pretty pictures with it!
He even drew pictures on our wells!

Prince: Oh, Dragon!
Our town doesn't look drab anymore.

Princess: It looks like a dream!

People: Hooray for Dragon!
Play the horns!
Bang the drums!

Narrator: The people asked Dragon to stay.
And the town got a new name—Dreamville!

✳ The End ✳

In the Flower Garden

Characters

Floyd (a caterpillar)   Rose Flower
Daisy Flower   Lily Flower

Floyd: I am a sad little caterpillar.

Daisy Flower: What's wrong, Floyd?

Floyd: I love the flower garden.
But there is one flaw.
I cannot see the flowers!

Rose Flower: That doesn't make sense.
Flowers are all around you!

Floyd: But I am flat on the ground.
I can only see stems.
I wish I weren't a caterpillar.

Lily Flower: What would you rather be?

Floyd: If I were a flea,
I could jump in the air.
Then I could see the flowers!

Daisy Flower: But someone could come
and flick you away.

25 Fun Phonics Plays for Beginning Readers © 2009 by Pamela Chanko, Scholastic Teaching Resources

Floyd: If I were a firefly,
I could flash my light.
Then I could see the flowers!

Rose Flower: But your spark could flicker out.

Floyd: If I were a bird,
I could fly up high.
Then I could see the flowers!

Lily Flower: But you could get lost in the flock.

Floyd: I'll never be able to see the flowers.
I feel like a flop!
I need to be alone now.

Daisy Flower: Floyd has been gone a long time.

Floyd: Daisy! Rose! Lily!
Look up here!

Rose Flower: Floyd! You have wings to flap!

Lily Flower: You can float in the air!

Floyd: I can flit and flutter about!
I can see the flowers!
The flower garden is beautiful!

**Daisy, Rose,
and Lily Flower:** Yes, it's the perfect place for a butterfly!

✳ The End ✳

Snail Has the Sniffles

Characters

Snail Snapping Turtle
Snowy Owl Snake

Snail: Sniff, sniff. Ah-CHOO!

Snowy Owl: Snail, you have the sniffles.
You should be in bed.

Snapping Turtle: Snowy Owl is right, Snail.
Go to bed, and make it snappy!

Snail: All right. Ah-CHOO!

Snowy Owl: You can snuggle this blanket.

Snapping Turtle: You can snooze on this pillow.

Snail: Thank you. Ah-CHOO!

Snowy Owl: Poor Snail can't stop sneezing.

Snapping Turtle: He's asleep now.
I can hear him snoring.

Snowy Owl: Let's make snow-pea soup for him!

Snail: Snore. Snort. Snuffle. - - - - - ➤

25 Fun Phonics Plays for Beginning Readers © 2009 by Pamela Chanko, Scholastic Teaching Resources

Snake: Snail is asleep.
I smell snow-pea soup.
I will sneak in and snatch it!

Snowy Owl: Stop snooping around, Snake!

Snapping Turtle: Oh, no! We are out of snow peas!

Snake: I have snow peas in my garden.
I will snip some for you.
Then can I share the soup?

Snowy Owl: Yes! Thank you, Snake!

Snapping Turtle: Look! Snail is awake.

Snail: I smell snow-pea soup!
My favorite!

All: Mmmm, yummy!

Snake: I will not be sneaky anymore.
Sharing with friends is fun!

**Snowy Owl and
Snapping Turtle:** Good for you, Snake!

Snail: Thanks for taking care of me.
I feel much better now.

Snake: Sniff, sniff. Ah-CHOO!

Snail: Uh-oh. Sorry, Snake.
Sometimes friends share sniffles, too!

✳ The End ✳

The Spiders Speak Up

Characters

Kids	Sparky Spider
Spanky Spider	Spencer Spider

Kids: Eek! A spider!

Spanky Spider: Don't you like spiders?

Kids: No, they are spooky!

Sparky Spider: We need to speak
to you about that.
We are not spooky.

Kids: You're not?

Spencer Spider: No! Spiders are special!

Kids: How?

Spanky Spider: We spin beautiful webs.

Sparky Spider: We use silk strings
that are longer than spaghetti.

Spencer Spider: Our webs sparkle in the sun.

Kids: But spider webs are sticky.

Spanky Spider: Is that why people spoil them?

Sparky Spider: We spend a lot of time
spinning our webs.

Spencer Spider: We work and work
until our spinners are sore.

Kids: We're sorry.
We didn't know.
We're glad you spoke up!

Spanky Spider: Hey! That's a great idea!

**Spencer and
Sparky Spider:**   What?

Spanky Spider: We will give a speech in town!

Spencer Spider: We will say how special we are!

Sparky Spider: Then we'll march in a spider parade!

Kids: We can have a Special Spider Day.
And we'll never call you spooky again!

❋ The End ❋

Starring Stan and Stella

Characters

Stella   Stan

Stella: What are you doing, Stan?

Stan: I'm practicing for the dance contest.
But I'm not the best dancer.
I'm stiff and I stumble.
I step on my own feet!

Stella: Ouch! That stings.

Stan: Watch this.
You see?
I can hardly stand up!
I stink at dancing!

Stella: Stop saying that, Stan.
Stay still and I will teach you.
Are you ready to start?

Stan: I'm ready!

Stella: Step, stamp, stamp.
Stomp, step, step.
Twist, stomp, twist.

25 Fun Phonics Plays for Beginning Readers © 2009 by Pamela Chankò, Scholastic Teaching Resources

Stan: I'm lost.
I can't do it that fast.

Stella: First, take a step.
Then, do a stamp.
Last, twist around.

Stan: I'm stuck!
I'm just no good at this stuff.

Stella: You almost have it!
Trust me!
Keep steady, now.

Stan: Step, stamp, stamp.
Stomp, step, step.
Twist, stomp, twist.
I did it!

Stella: You see?
Now I will teach you a stunt.
You can do those steps
on the stairs!

Stan: Those stairs look steep, Stella.

Stella: At least try it!
Come on!

Both: Step, stamp, stamp.
Stomp, step, step.
Twist, stomp, twist.

Stella: Now you are dancing with style!
You are a very good student.

Stan: Well, you made me stick with it.
Enter the contest with me!

Stella: You want to do the steps together?

Stan: Yes! We'll stun the judges!

Stella: We'll steal the show!

Stan: We'll be Stan and Stella,
stars of the stage!

Both: And the rest will be history!

✳ The End ✳

 25 Fun Phonics Plays for Beginning Readers © 2009 by Pamela Chanko, Scholastic Teaching Resources

Trash for Treasure

Characters

Tracy Trent

Tracy: Hi, Trent.
What's in that bag?

Trent: I am taking my old toys
to the trash.
What's in your bag, Tracy?

Tracy: I am doing the same thing!

Trent: Let's look in each other's bags.

Tracy: Okay.
I like your toy tractor.

Trent: I like your toy trailer.

Tracy: I'll trade my trailer
for your tractor.

Trent: Okay!

Tracy: I was really tired of my trailer.
I'm glad you want it!

Trent: I was really tired of my tractor.
I'm glad you want it!
I like your trains.

Tracy: I like your trucks.

Trent: I'll trade my trucks
for your trains.

Trent: Great!

Tracy: I was bored with my trains.
But you will have fun with them.

Trent: I was bored with my trucks.
But you will have fun with them.

Tracy: Hey, we traded everything!
My trash bag is empty!

Trent: Mine, too!
And now I have new toys
to try out.

Tracy: Me, too!
I will put them
in my toy treasure chest.

Trent: We both went out with trash.

Both: But we came back with treasure!

✳ The End ✳

25 Fun Phonics Plays for Beginning Readers © 2009 by Pamela Chanko, Scholastic Teaching Resources